THE 4 STAGES OF A

CHEATING MAN

UNDERSTANDING THE MIND THAT CHEATS

MANUEL V. JOHNSON

THE 4 STAGES OF A CHEATING MAN

Tampa, Florida
Published in the United States of America

ISBN: 978-0-9861430-8-3

Disclaimer:
This book is based on personal observations, opinions, and research intended for informational and educational purposes only. It is not a substitute for professional counseling, therapy, or legal advice. The author and publisher make no guarantees about the outcomes of applying the ideas discussed herein. Readers should use their own judgment and, when necessary, consult qualified professionals regarding their individual situations. Any resemblance to actual persons, living or dead, is purely coincidental.

TABLE OF CONTENTS

THE CHEATING PROGRAM

Introduction

Your're here because something in you still aches for answers. Maybe you've been lied to, betrayed, or left wondering how the man who said he loved you could still hurt you. Maybe you've forgiven him, but deep down, you still don't understand him.

Whatever brought you here, I know you're not looking for pity. You want clarity. You want to understand why men do what they do. You want to see the patterns before they play out again.

This book was written for that. It's not here to make you lose hope in love. It's here to help you see it for what it really is. To help you understand the mind of a man who cheats, not to justify it, but to expose it. Because once you understand how a man thinks, you can stop taking his actions personally. You stop blaming yourself for his choices.

The truth is, a man's betrayal says more about his lack of discipline than your worth. But when you understand the stages he moves through, the reasons he gives, and the patterns he repeats, everything starts to make sense. The confusion begins to fade. The fog clears.

This book should bring you that level of clarity. It should help you see him differently - not through the lens of what he said, but through the reality of who he is. And once you understand that, you'll finally know how to protect your peace, your time, and your heart.

.

THE 4 STAGES OF A
CHEATING MAN
UNDERSTANDING THE MIND THAT CHEATS

CHEATING: 101

The Seed

Cheating does not start with the act. It starts with the mindset.

Long before your man lays down with another woman, something is already happening in his mind, in his habits, and in what he was taught to believe about being a man.

From the time many boys are young, they are taught that manhood is proven by how many women they can sleep with. It is not just about desire; it is about ego.

The more women they can get, the more they feel like they matter. That becomes the scoreboard. That becomes validation.

You can see it everywhere. It is in the songs that glorify having multiple women and brag about taking another man's girl. It is in the lyrics that make sex sound like a competition and loyalty sound like weakness. So by the time he is old enough to fall in love, he has already learned to measure himself by how many hearts he can touch, not how well he can keep one.

You see it on screen too. In movies, the man who gets all the women is almost always the one with confidence, danger, and charm. He is the rapper in the video, the rebel in the film, the man everyone else wants to be. He is cool. He is admired. He is desired. And because of that, young men grow up believing that having many women is what makes a man powerful.

The opposite image rarely gets any attention. The man who is faithful to one woman, who minds his business, who stays consistent, is often portrayed as dull or uninteresting. In the world's eyes, he is not "the man." He is just the one who settled down.

In other words, when culture keeps painting loyalty as boring and promiscuity as powerful, it confuses a man's sense of identity. The boy who grows up obsessed with being cool becomes the man who fears being overlooked. He does not want to be seen as lame, so he chases attention. But the truth is, the man who can love one woman and stay grounded in that love is not lame at all. That is strength. That is control. The problem is that society has not made that look cool yet.

Now the same messages that once lived in music videos and movies are everywhere online. Social media has turned validation into a daily fix. Every like, comment, and message feeds the same need for attention that started in him years ago. He does not have to approach women in person anymore to feel wanted; he can scroll and get it instantly. Validation is no longer earned; it is easily available. And the more it is available, the harder it becomes to let go of.

The world keeps rewarding men for being wanted, not for being stable. It teaches them how to chase women but not how to value them.

In other words, the problem does not start in the relationship. It starts in the culture. Men are not born this way; they are built this way. And until a man unlearns that conditioning, he will always be at war with himself, torn between the man he wants to be and the one the world taught him to become.

But the danger runs deeper than habits or ego. Once a man keeps feeding that pattern of chasing lust, attention, and pride, he starts to open spiritual doors he does not even realize exist. Every time he entertains those temptations, he invites more of that energy into his life. The music, the validation, and the constant desire to be seen all create space for darker influences to move.

Those demons do not always show up wearing horns. Sometimes they look like opportunity. Sometimes they sound like approval. But their goal is the same: to separate a man from his purpose, his peace, and his discipline.

And when a man loses discipline, everything else follows. That is when the habits turn into addictions. That is when the pride turns into blindness. And that is when cheating becomes more than a choice; it becomes a pattern he cannot break.

The next section dives into that pattern, the spiritual pull, the lack of discipline, and the insecurity that keeps it alive. Because once you understand the forces working in him and around him, you will see cheating for what it really is: not just betrayal, but bondage.

So let's start where it all begins, the roots.

CHEATING: 102

The Roots

The Emotional Root

Every act of cheating has a beginning, but not every beginning looks the same. Some start from curiosity. Some start from pride. Some start from pain. But deep down, most forms of cheating come from the same root - insecurity.

Many cheaters are not driven by lust. They are driven by fear. They chase acceptance. They want to feel admired, chosen, and seen. When that feeling fades inside the relationship, they do not know how to speak up, so they go looking for it somewhere else.

A lot of people think cheating is all about sex, but for many men it is about trying to feel significant again. When a man starts believing that who he really is will not be enough to keep someone's attention, he hides behind an image. He avoids conflict to keep the peace. He says what she wants to hear. He shapes himself into what he thinks she will keep loving. But that version of him is not real. It is survival.

In other words:
- He has been faking peace to keep her happy.
- He has been suppressing his real emotions and pretending everything is fine.
- He is doing things he does not want to do just to maintain her approval.
- But because that version of him is not the real him, the relationship starts to feel empty.
- And instead of confronting the truth that he has been pretending, he goes outside the relationship to feel "seen" again.

- The problem is not that she stopped showing value. It is that he built the connection on performance, not truth.

So no, this kind of cheating does not come from arrogance. It comes from fear - fear of being himself and losing approval. But here is the truth: when a man spends his energy pretending to be perfect, he ends up losing the very connection he was trying to protect.

Now let's look deeper at that fear. A lot of men were never taught how to process emotional needs in a healthy way. They learned early that vulnerability makes you look weak. So they grow up hiding pain instead of healing from it. When a man does not know how to express what he feels, he learns to replace emotion with distraction. Some drink. Some stay busy at work. Some cheat.

In other words:
- Cheating becomes a distraction from reality.
- It is easier to chase a new moment than face what is broken inside.
- It is not about finding someone better than his woman. It is about avoiding his true self.

And that is where the emotional confusion begins. He convinces himself he is "missing something" in the relationship when what he is really missing is self-awareness. His cheating does not solve the problem; it magnifies it. Because once he crosses that line, he has to live with the guilt of what he did and the emptiness that made him do it.

To his partner, it feels like betrayal. To him, it feels like relief...for a moment. Then the shame creeps back in, and he starts needing more of what created the problem in order to silence the guilt. It is a dangerous cycle: validation, guilt, distraction, repeat.

In other words:
- He cheats to escape his emotions.
- The guilt drives him to cheat again.
- The more he does it, the emptier he becomes.
- The emptier he becomes, the more validation he needs. Which keeps him seeking that next high.

And here is where some women get confused. They think if they love him harder, he will stop. They think if they can show him he is worth something, he will see what he already has. But insecurity does not heal through love alone. It heals through awareness, truth, and discipline.

Until a man faces the reasons behind his fear, he will keep repeating the same behavior. You can love him, pray for him, support him, but you cannot heal what he refuses to acknowledge.

Before a man ever cheats physically, he cheats emotionally by betraying honesty, peace, and self-control. He betrays his own standards long before he betrays yours.

In other words:
- Cheating begins in his mindset, not in the bed.
- It is a symptom of confusion, not confidence.
- And until he learns who he is without validation, he will always need attention to survive.

That need for attention is what opens the next door - the spiritual one. Because once a man starts feeding his weakness instead of healing it, he creates space for darker energy to enter. The next part will go deeper into that side of the battle.

The Spiritual Root

Every relationship is fighting an invisible battle. You cannot see it, but you can feel it. You feel it when peace suddenly turns to tension for no reason. You feel it when temptation shows up out of nowhere. You feel it when a man starts slipping back into habits he promised he left behind. That is not coincidence. It is energy.

Some call it temptation. Others call it spiritual warfare. Whatever you call it, it is real. When a man allows lust, ego, and pride to guide him, he opens doors he does not understand. Every song he listens to, every image he watches, and every moment he entertains that energy, he is feeding something that wants to destroy him.

Temptation does not knock politely. It whispers. It waits for moments of weakness, loneliness, stress, or boredom, and then it plants thoughts. The thought becomes curiosity. Curiosity becomes justification. And before long, that justification becomes action.

In other words:

- Temptation rarely forces; it convinces.
- It does not break the door down; it waits for you to leave it unlocked.
- Once it gets in, it makes you think it was your idea all along.

A lot of women do not realize this, but when their man is fighting temptation, they are fighting it too. They are both at war with unseen energy. Lust does not just target him; it targets the bond between them. That is why a relationship built only on feelings will struggle when the spiritual pressure comes. Both people have to guard their minds, their hearts, and their energy.

When those temptations show up, they do not always look evil. Sometimes they look like curiosity. Sometimes they sound like freedom. Sometimes they come disguised as confidence. But the end result is always the same: division, guilt, and distance.

In other words:

- Every couple is being tested.
- Temptation is not about pleasure; it is about separation.
- You are either protecting your peace or feeding your weakness.

Now let us talk about one of the biggest unseen influences, which is porn. Many people think watching porn is harmless. Some women even believe that their man watching it keeps him from cheating. It sounds logical, but it is a lie. Porn does not satisfy lust; it strengthens it. It feeds the same spiritual energy that pushes men toward infidelity.

When a man watches porn, he is not just looking at a screen. He is programming his brain to crave newness. He is training himself to desire variety instead of intimacy. Over time, the woman he has begins to feel familiar instead of exciting. That is how spiritual decay begins - in private moments, on a glowing screen, in silence.

Think of it like this. Eating a plate of ribs is like sleeping with another woman. But watching porn is like grabbing a rib and then licking your fingers without eating it. You may not have eaten the ribs, but you are still tasting them. You are still feeding the craving. The more you stay in that space, the stronger the urge becomes, until eventually you stop watching and start acting.

In other words:

- Porn is not release; it is rehearsal.
- It teaches the body to respond to fantasy, not reality.
- It trains the spirit to accept impurity as entertainment.

That is why spiritual accountability matters. When a man believes that no one sees him, he is most vulnerable to temptation. But when he remembers that God sees him, even in the dark, that awareness changes everything. It shifts his choices from impulse to responsibility.

Temptation always hides in privacy. The phone in his hand, the computer screen at night, and the silence when no one is around are the battlefields. If a man cannot hold himself accountable in private, public promises will never hold weight.

Awareness is the first step toward change, but awareness alone is not enough. You cannot defeat spiritual habits with willpower. You have to replace them. That is where discipline begins.

You cannot cast out a habit; you have to crowd it out. If you remove something destructive, you must fill that space with something positive. If a man smokes every time he drives home, he has to replace that moment with a different focus, something that feeds peace instead of feeding weakness.

For example, I once replaced smoking on my long drives with brushing my hair. I wanted waves at the time, so I brushed for that entire hour instead of smoking. It sounds small, but it worked. My hands stayed busy, my mind stayed occupied, and my spirit stayed calmer. The goal is not perfection. The goal is replacement. And sure enough, I'm now 11 years smoke-free.

In other words:
- You cannot defeat temptation by staring at it.
- You overcome it by changing what you feed.
- What you do repeatedly becomes what you desire.
- Replace the desire and the habit loses power.

This principle applies to everything. Replace gossip with gratitude. Replace lust with purpose. Replace secrecy with honesty. That is the spiritual foundation of discipline. You do not just resist darkness; you fill yourself with light.

Discipline is not punishment. It is protection. It guards the soul from influences that want to pull it apart. When a man forgets that, he becomes easy prey. He starts believing he can handle temptation alone. He tells himself he can stop anytime and that he is still in control. But control without discipline is an illusion.

Temptation does not care how strong you look; it attacks how focused you are. If a man's focus is scattered, temptation wins before the battle even begins.

That is why spiritual discipline matters so much. It is not about religion; it is about awareness. It is knowing that energy, intention, and attention are always at war. It is understanding that lust does not just aim to make him cheat; it aims to make him forget who he is.

Every relationship has moments when both people are tempted to act on emotion, frustration, or desire. Those moments are not proof that love is gone. They are reminders that love must be guarded. And the guard is discipline.

The next part of this chapter goes deeper into that, showing that real masculinity is not about how many desires a man has, but how many he can master. Because it is not about the temptation that finds him; it is about the discipline that saves him.

The Discipline Root

Discipline is not about control. It is about alignment. It is a man bringing his emotions, desires, and impulses into agreement with his purpose. Without discipline, purpose is just potential. Without discipline, love is just a feeling waiting to fade. A man can be talented, ambitious, loving, and spiritual, but if he lacks discipline, he will lose to his own habits. He will be loyal in public and reckless in private. He will pray for peace but still feed the same chaos that steals it.

That is why discipline is the foundation of maturity. It is not something a man finds; it is something he builds. Every man has urges. That is normal. But not every man knows what to do with them. A mature man does not deny that those urges exist. He simply learns to rule them. The problem is not attraction. The problem is obedience to attraction.

A man without discipline becomes a slave to his own impulses. He stops making choices and starts reacting. He stops leading and starts following desire. The more he follows, the weaker his will becomes.

In other words:
- Attraction is not the issue. Action is.
- Discipline does not erase desire; it teaches timing.
- A man who can control himself can protect everything he loves.

When a man learns discipline, it changes how he moves. He thinks before he speaks. He pauses before he acts. He recognizes when his flesh is louder than his spirit. That awareness does not make him perfect, but it keeps him accountable. Every man is one decision away from peace or regret. Discipline is what separates the two.

You cannot build discipline by talking about it. You build it through repetition, by choosing what is right until it becomes natural. As I mentioned before, you cannot simply stop bad habits; you have to replace them. If a man constantly argues, he can start replacing reaction with silence. If he scrolls through temptation online, he can replace it with study or prayer. If he stays up watching lustful videos, he can replace that hour with reflection, journaling, or creating something that builds him.

The key is not suppression. It is substitution. When you replace something toxic with something healthy, the mind begins to crave what strengthens it instead of what destroys it.

In other words:

- Discipline is not about saying "no" once. It is about saying "yes" to something better every time.
- You cannot remove weakness; you must starve it.
- Every strong man had to master repetition before he mastered control.

Most men think freedom means doing whatever they want. But real freedom is being able to say no and still feel powerful. Freedom without discipline is a slow form of destruction.

Discipline is what makes love consistent. It keeps a man from saying things in anger that he will regret in peace. It keeps him from chasing temporary pleasure when he already has permanent value at home. It keeps him from blaming temptation for what was really a lack of preparation.

If a man cannot control himself, he cannot lead a family, build a future, or protect what he loves. Leadership starts with self-control. You cannot lead anyone until you can lead yourself.

A man who lacks discipline will always have an excuse. He will blame stress, opportunity, or loneliness. But a man with discipline will always have a standard. He knows that what feels good in the moment will cost him peace later. He understands that love requires sacrifice, and commitment requires consistency.

In other words:
- Weak men chase comfort.
- Strong men chase purpose.
- Discipline is what turns purpose into progress.

If a man cheats, it is not always because he does not love his partner. It is because he does not love his peace enough to protect it. Discipline is protection. It is how a man guards his relationship from the parts of himself that still crave attention.

But discipline is not built overnight. It starts small, one decision at a time. Just like a body grows from daily workouts, discipline grows from daily choices. Every time a man chooses control over impulse, his spirit gets stronger. Control over impulse!

A faithful man is not weak. He is focused. He understands that every time he says no to something that could destroy him, he says yes to everything that will build him.

When a man reaches that level of awareness, he no longer needs to prove his manhood through attention. His validation comes from mastery. He does not need to be chased or praised. He has peace, and peace is the reward for discipline.

Discipline is not perfection. It is protection. It does not mean he will never feel tempted. It means he is prepared when temptation comes.

Final Words

This is the mindset of a cheater, where he stands mentally, spiritually, and emotionally. Everything he does in his relationships comes from this foundation. His culture has shaped his ego, temptation has shaped his habits, and the lack of discipline has shaped his decisions. But cheating does not begin and end with a single act. It is a process that moves through stages. Some men never leave the first one because they never grow. Others slowly begin to change, not because time matures them, but because pain, reflection, and awareness start to open their eyes.

The stages that follow show what that growth looks like and how a man moves from being fully committed to cheating to finally being ready to stop.

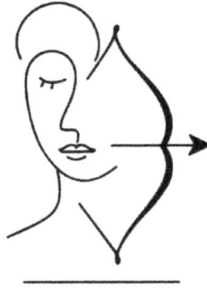

STAGE 1

THE HUNTER

This is the man who is already in a relationship but still lives like he is single. He tells people he is committed, but his actions show otherwise. The Hunter does not cheat because of temptation; he cheats because he already planned to. He does not see commitment as a reason to stop pursuing women. To him, having a girlfriend is just having a main base to return to after he has been out playing.

If you were to sit in on one of his conversations with his boys, you would hear it. They might ask, *"So, you're locking this one down or still moving how you move?"* and he will laugh and say something like, *"Yeah, she's my main one."* That one line tells you everything. The word "main" implies there are others. The Hunter uses language like that without even thinking about it because in his mind, multiple women are normal. Commitment does not mean loyalty. It just means priority.

The Hunter still chases. He is the type to walk up to a woman in a grocery store, compliment her, and get her number before he reaches the next aisle. He slides into DMs with confidence, starts conversations with strangers, and flirts everywhere he goes. For him, it is not just about sleeping with someone. It is about proving he can still attract whoever he wants. The pursuit is the addiction, not the woman.

He also chases with his presence. He stares too long, smiles too hard, and makes jokes that sound harmless but are really small invitations. Even at work, at the gym, or at a family event, he finds a way to turn a simple interaction into a test of his charm. He will flirt with the waitress, compliment the cashier, and engage in "friendly" banter with women he meets. Every time he gets a smile back, he feels more alive.

When The Hunter gets into a new relationship, he does not delete numbers, block old flings, or end connections. He just goes quiet for a while. The women he used to mess with are still there, the ex he checks on "just to make sure she's okay," the coworker he flirts with on lunch breaks, the woman at church he compliments every Sunday. He keeps them all close enough to reach but far enough to hide. He has a roster of women – new and old. He doesn't always have to start fresh or build trust. The door was never closed to begin with in many cases.

But even with all those old doors open, he still never stops looking for new ones. The Hunter never starts over. He just adds on. The old women stay in his phone for comfort, and the new women feed his ego. He calls it having options, but what he really has is a collection. He does not delete names or numbers. He just rearranges them. Every time he gets a new woman, he feels like he has leveled up, even though he is still running in circles.

In other words:

- The Hunter does not cut ties; he pauses them.
- He chases new women to prove his worth.

If you looked through his phone, you would see patterns. Messages deleted halfway through the thread. Saved numbers under nicknames or emojis. Contacts that have not been called in months but can be texted at any moment. He might tell his girl he does not use social media much, but he is active in DMs she will never see. He scrolls through women's stories, reacts to pictures, or drops a heart just to keep the connection warm.

The Hunter does not stumble into cheating. He prepares for it. He creates space for it in his routine. When he goes out, he keeps his phone face down on the table. When he is out late, he has an excuse ready before he even gets questioned. If his partner asks who he was talking to, he turns it into a debate about trust. Every defense is pre-rehearsed because this is a lifestyle, not an accident.

He is confident, charming, and social. He knows how to make a woman feel special, but it is not because he genuinely wants to connect. It is because he is practiced. The compliments, the timing, the humor, the stories, they have all been used before. He studies what works and repeats it. When women say, *"He just gets me,"* it is because he has learned how to read emotions and respond in a way that feels personal. But none of it is rooted in truth. It is all performance.

In other words:

- He is not flirting by accident; he is following a script.
- His charm is rehearsed, not authentic.
- He knows what to say because he has said it before.

The Hunter's circle of friends keeps him stuck. He is surrounded by men who think like him, men who laugh about cheating and share stories like they are highlights. They take pride in how many women they can pull. If one of them tries to slow down or be faithful, the others clown him for it. These are not the type of men who push each other toward growth. They push each other toward ego.

Women often confuse his consistency with loyalty, but the truth is that The Hunter is only consistent with his habits. He knows how to apologize when caught, how to cry on cue, and how to sound sincere without ever meaning it. He will say, *"You're the one I want,"* but that sentence only lasts until he is bored again. He does not chase new women out of need. He does it because each conquest feeds his ego.

For The Hunter, every woman is a trophy. Each one represents a victory, a confirmation that he still has it. That is why he rarely hides his evidence completely. He might keep a pair of panties tucked away, or videos, or old pictures on his phone. Those things are proof. Proof that he can still get what he wants when he wants it. That is why so many Hunters get caught. It is not just carelessness. It is pride.

He does not delete numbers because it feels like throwing away a win. He does not clear his photo gallery because he likes scrolling through his own success. Every woman becomes a memory of validation. When you understand that, you understand why catching him does not always stop him. You can take away the woman, but you cannot take away the need to prove himself.

When a man lives in this stage, he is not cheating for adventure. He is cheating for identity. He tells himself he can love his girl and still sleep with other women. He says, *"I'm just being a man,"* as if manhood requires deception. He knows it is wrong, but he convinces himself it is harmless. He will even say, *"I'd rather cheat than leave,"* as if that is some form of loyalty.

In other words:
- He believes loyalty means not leaving, not staying faithful.
- He sees cheating as self-maintenance, not betrayal.
- He defines manhood by how much attention he can attract.

When you confront The Hunter, he flips the conversation. If you question him, you become the problem. He will say you are insecure or that you do not trust him. If you bring up specifics, he will say you are overreacting or accuse you of snooping. The more you push, the more defensive he gets. He uses confusion as a weapon because confusion buys him time. The goal is not to win the argument; it is to wear you out so you stop asking.

At his core, The Hunter is insecure. He thrives on being desired because he does not know how to feel valuable without it. The more women want him, the more powerful he feels. But the satisfaction does not last. It fades within days, sometimes hours. That is why he has to keep chasing it. He is addicted to the attention. It is his drug.

You will notice that men in this stage often repeat patterns. They cheat, feel guilty, apologize, then cheat again. It is not the cheating that controls them; it is the cycle. The guilt becomes part of the process. It is how they reset emotionally. They do wrong, they promise to do better, then they slip again. The apology gives them temporary peace, but not real change.

In other words:
- The Hunter's guilt is routine, not repentance.
- His apology is part of the cheating cycle.

- He needs forgiveness just enough to cheat again.

Spiritually, he is disconnected. Every time he cheats, he feels a small tug of guilt, but he has learned to silence it. He might pray after he gets caught or promise God he will stop, but those prayers are panic, not conviction. He knows right from wrong, but right feels too quiet, and wrong feels too exciting. The thrill makes him feel alive.

When he talks to his friends, they usually reinforce his behavior. They laugh about cheating stories, swap lies, share nudes of women and tell him he is just being a man. That kind of support makes him believe that cheating is harmless as long as no one finds out. What he does not realize is that every lie is disconnecting him from his purpose. He cannot lead his household because he is living two lives. He cannot grow because he is stuck managing lies instead of building trust.

In other words:
- He is surrounded by men who normalize cheating.

- He is disconnected from purpose and discipline.
- He confuses excitement with happiness.

Most Hunters stay in this stage for years. They slow down only when something shakes them, a breakup, getting caught, losing someone who truly mattered, or simply getting older. The thrill starts to fade. The lies get harder to juggle. The women do not excite him like they used to. That is when he starts to slow down, not because he has changed, but because the energy to keep lying runs out.

Still, not every man grows from that. Some will stay Hunters forever, stuck in the same cycle, blaming women, and calling their own behavior normal. Other men will start to feel that emptiness more deeply and begin to question themselves. They will wonder why the excitement does not feel the same anymore, why the guilt hits harder, and why peace feels harder to find. That is when the next shift begins.

For the few who start that internal process, who begin to feel tired of their own habits, the next stage starts to form. Not real growth yet, but hesitation. He is no longer chasing as hard. He is slowing down, but not because he is disciplined. It is because the thrill is fading. That slowing is where Stage 2 begins, the stage of *The Opportunist*.

STAGE 2

THE OPPORTUNIST

The Opportunist is a man in transition, but not transformation. He has slowed down, but not matured. He has not grown wiser, only wearier. He is not chasing women anymore, yet he has not learned how to close the doors behind him.

To outsiders, he seems more grounded. He looks calmer, speaks softer, and acts more reserved. He will tell you things like, *"I'm done playing games,"* or *"I don't move like that anymore."* It sounds like progress. But it is not peace that calmed him; it is exhaustion. The energy that used to fuel his chase has faded, but his desire has not.

He does not flirt as boldly as before, but the instinct remains. If a woman from his past texts him *"Hey stranger,"* he does not ignore it. He replies, *"Wow, been a minute. How you been?"* He calls that "harmless conversation," yet he knows exactly where it can lead. His justification is simple: he did not start it. In his mind, not chasing means he is faithful, even if he still entertains temptation.

In other words:
- He has not changed; he has only slowed down.
- He does not pursue, but he still responds.
- He measures growth by cheating inactivity, not integrity.

The Opportunist believes that because he no longer goes out of his way to cheat, he is somehow reformed. What he fails to see is that temptation does not require effort; it only needs availability. He may not chase new women, but he keeps himself within reach of the old ones. He keeps their numbers saved, their messages hidden, and their access open.

He has developed new habits that look like boundaries, but they are really barriers for show. He no longer goes out clubbing every weekend, but he still flirts at work. He does not slide into DMs, but he still likes certain pictures late at night. He no longer meets new women in public, but he keeps up "friendly" conversations with old ones. The cheating has shifted from pursuit to opportunity.

He has also become more cautious about who he hangs out with. The reckless nights and random parties are behind him, but the people he still spends time with all cheat too. They normalize it, joke about it, and make him feel like he is still part of something familiar. Even if he is not chasing women anymore, his circle reminds him that cheating is acceptable. Their habits feed his comfort.

In other words:
- He avoids change by staying around people who never grow.

- His environment still justifies his behavior.
- He protects the same lifestyle, just with fewer witnesses.

The Opportunist still values validation. He does not chase it, but he quietly craves it. He posts photos hoping for compliments, shares subtle quotes hoping someone slides into his inbox, and makes himself visible without being obvious. He wants to appear content but still be noticed. His self-worth still depends on how women react to him.

This stage is where *emotional cheating* often begins. He may not be having sex with anyone else, but he is giving emotional energy away. He starts sharing parts of himself that should belong only to his partner. He vents to other women about his problems. He opens up about stress, frustrations, or how misunderstood he feels. Those conversations build emotional intimacy without accountability. It starts as friendship, then turns into comfort, and eventually crosses a line.

If you confront him, he will say, *"We're just cool,"* or, *"You're overthinking it."* But the truth is simple: if the roles were reversed, he would not tolerate it.

The Opportunist sees himself as controlled, but he is really calculating. He knows what to say and what to hide. He deletes messages immediately after reading them. He clears call logs, changes names in his phone, or uses secret apps to stay undetected. He thinks that because he is careful, he is better. But cheating quietly is still cheating.

He calls his silence maturity. In reality, it is strategy. He has become more efficient, not more faithful.

He convinces himself that as long as he is not chasing, he is doing better. But he does not realize that cheating is not about pursuit; it is about permission. His problem was never effort; it was entitlement. He still feels entitled to emotional attention and validation outside his relationship. He still enjoys the power of knowing he can have it.

In his mind, he is not like his old self anymore. He tells himself, *"At least I'm not wild like I used to be."* He compares his current behavior to his past chaos, and that comparison comforts him. But the standard is wrong. You cannot call it growth if you are still moving in the same direction, only slower.

When The Opportunist cheats, it often happens in moments of opportunity, not planning. A friendly conversation at work turns into lunch. A joke turns into flirting. A touch lingers too long. He does not seek it, but he does not stop it either. He tells himself, *"It just happened,"* but nothing ever just happens. Opportunity needs access, and he has never stopped giving access.

His partner begins to notice the emotional distance. He is home more, but less present. He smiles less, talks less, and avoids deeper conversations. She can feel something is off but cannot prove it. That is because his cheating no longer looks like cheating. It has moved from physical to emotional, from reckless to restrained. He has become harder to catch because his lies are now subtle.

Spiritually, he is split. He knows better, but he does not want to lose the thrill completely. He still wants to feel desired, but now he wants to feel respected too. He is trying to live in both worlds, the thrill of the old life and the peace of the new one, but both cannot exist together.

This is why the Opportunist eventually feels trapped. He is not happy cheating, but he is not ready to stop either. He prays for strength but avoids accountability. He tells God, *"I'm trying,"* yet still keeps every door open for another woman. He has not learned to tell himself no.

When a man has not mastered discipline, it does not matter how much he claims to have changed. He will always be one opportunity away from falling again.

In other words:
- The Opportunist mistakes exhaustion for growth.
- He is not chasing peace; he is avoiding guilt.
- He thinks less action means progress, but it really just means delay.

What he does not realize is that slowing down is not the same as changing. You cannot outgrow sin by walking slower in it. Until he confronts why he needs external validation and replaces it with internal value, he will never be free.

That is where the next stage begins, not with healing but with awareness. He starts to see patterns in himself, starts to notice that his behavior no longer satisfies him, and begins to realize that cheating has lost its flavor. But instead of stopping, he tries to control it. He begins to play the game with precision, believing he can cheat smarter, quieter, and safer.

That is when *The Strategist* is born.

STAGE 3

THE STRATEGIST

The Strategist is not the loud, reckless man he once was. He doesn't brag about cheating, and he doesn't chase women openly. His ego isn't loud anymore. It's quiet, calculated, and hidden behind control. To him, chaos is for amateurs. He's learned to cheat with order.

Unlike the Hunter, who chased women out of ego, or the Opportunist, who cheated out of habit, the Strategist cheats out of ideology. He believes cheating can be done responsibly, like managing a secret job on the side. In his mind, there's nothing wrong with doing what *all men do*, as long as he keeps it clean.

He tells himself discipline isn't about denying what he wants. It's about controlling when and how he gets it. So he *plans* his infidelity with precision. No random flings. No messy entanglements. He studies every situation before he moves. He picks women carefully, the quiet ones, the ones with something to lose. Married women. Single mothers. Professionals. Women who won't talk.

He uses secret calculator apps that look harmless but open to private photos and hidden contacts once a code is entered. He often memorizes numbers so he doesn't have to save them. He deletes messages, then empties the deleted folder too. By the time he gets home, there's no trace of what he's done.

When he's out of town, he's in his element. The distance gives him cover. He flirts, meets up, and tells himself it's harmless because no one will ever know. Then, on the drive home, he deletes the evidence, puts on his ring, and plays the loving man again.

He sees this as mastery. He believes he's evolved past the mistakes of his younger self. To him, the Hunter was sloppy. The Opportunist was careless. But he, the Strategist, is disciplined. He cheats with structure, boundaries, and self-control, as if sin can be perfected through organization.

In other words:

- He calls cheating "discipline" because he believes being organized about it makes him better than men who are sloppy
- He tells himself things like, *"At least I'm honest about who I am,"* or, *"I don't mess with just anyone."* He believes that setting rules around cheating makes it more acceptable.
- He doesn't realize the real problem isn't the mess he avoids but the mindset he protects. By convincing himself he's managing it, he ignores the truth that he's still choosing it.

He has a system for everything. He knows when to text, when to stop, and when to pull away before emotions get involved. If a woman starts asking for too much, he cuts her off like she's a bad investment. He tells himself she knew the deal. He convinces himself he's protecting her feelings when really he's protecting his image.

He still believes he's a good man. He'll send money to help a woman pay her bills or buy her child's school shoes, and he'll say, *"She needed me."* He convinces himself he's spreading kindness. But in reality, he's feeding two ego, hers and his own.

At home, he plays his part well. He posts pictures, smiles in family photos, remembers anniversaries, and keeps up appearances. He knows that being seen together kills suspicion. His woman may even feel secure, unaware that the security she feels is part of his strategy.

To outsiders, he looks loyal. Inside, he's still divided. He's loyal to both worlds, the home that gives him identity and the secrets that give him control.

Spiritually, he's still trapped. His prayer life is shallow. When he prays, it's not for forgiveness, it's for cover. He doesn't ask God to help him change, only to help him not get caught. His faith is surface-deep, his peace counterfeit. He's living under the illusion that as long as his heart feels calm, God must understand. But that calm isn't peace. It's numbness. He tells himself he's "balanced." He says, *"I can love one and still care for another."* But that's not balance. It's brokenness that's learned how to look stable.

In other words:
- Spiritually, he's not growing, he's bargaining. He prays when he's scared, not when he's sorry. He thanks God for blessings but never asks for change, because change would cost him the life he's built.
- He thinks staying out of trouble equals peace, but real peace doesn't come from keeping secrets. It comes from surrendering them.
- He says things like, *"God knows my heart,"* as if that excuses what he does. But what God actually knows is that his heart isn't conflicted, it's comfortable.

He still surrounds himself with other men who think the same way. They talk in quiet circles, men who once were wild but now cheat in secret. They don't celebrate it, but they don't condemn it either. They call it "phases," "mistakes," "slips." They trade stories without guilt, each one reinforcing the other's lie that this is just what men do.

He no longer feels the rush of cheating. What used to feel powerful now feels mechanical. But he doesn't stop, because stopping would mean facing himself. So he keeps going, not for pleasure, but for identity. Cheating is how he maintains the illusion that he's still in control.

He's become the type of man who sins efficiently but sleeps peacefully. Not because he's innocent, but because he's mastered how to live with guilt. He no longer flinches when he lies. He no longer hesitates when he hides. His conscience is quiet because he's trained it to be.

In other words:
- He can go from one woman's house to another's bed and still come home calm, smiling, and present.

- He's trained his emotions to stay flat, so when his woman looks at him and asks if something's wrong, he can look her in the eye and say, *"Everything's fine."*
- The calm you see on his face isn't peace, it's numbness. And the more numb he gets, the easier it becomes to keep doing the same thing again.

But this stage cannot last forever. The Strategist doesn't realize that the same system that once made him feel powerful will soon drain him. The pressure to stay perfect begins to wear him down. His calm starts to feel like emptiness. His control starts to feel like a cage.

He grows tired. Not tired of cheating, but tired of maintaining the lie. He begins to crave peace, but he doesn't yet know what *real* peace feels like.

This is where the Strategist slows down. He hasn't changed; he's just drained. And that is how the Strategist becomes *The Settler*.

STAGE 4

THE SETTLER

The Settler is the man who's slowed down, not because he's changed, but because he's tired. He isn't chasing women. He isn't texting new ones or scrolling through DMs. He's not looking to cheat. That part of his life feels over. But his loyalty isn't built on conviction; it's built on circumstance.

He's faithful because nothing tempting has crossed his path. He believes he's matured, but what he calls growth is really distance from opportunity. If the timing, the place, and the mood ever lined up perfectly, he knows deep down he might still give in. He tells himself he wouldn't, but he's never been truly tested.

He's said no before. He's turned women down. Sometimes he even feels proud of that. But what he doesn't admit is that those moments were easy to resist. The woman wasn't his type, or he wasn't in the mood, or the situation wasn't private enough. When the perfect storm never comes, it's easy to believe the clouds of temptation are gone.

In other words:
- He thinks he's faithful but it's because the right situation hasn't come up yet. He hasn't had to fight temptation; he's just been away from it.
- He tells himself he's grown, but what's really happened is that life got quieter, not that he got stronger.
- His loyalty feels genuine, but it's not built on discipline. It's built on lack of opportunity. If the stars ever lined up just right, his old self could still show up.

He's calmer now, but the calm is shallow. It's the quiet that comes when a man's energy has burned out. His passion for chasing women is gone, but so is the fire that used to drive him to change. He's not restless; he's just numb.

His woman thinks she finally has the faithful version of him, and on the surface, she does. He works, comes home, keeps a routine. He doesn't flirt openly or stay out late. Yet every now and then, something inside him flickers; a glance, a laugh, a moment of attention from another woman. He doesn't seek it, but he notices it. He enjoys it just enough to remind himself he still could, if he wanted to.

He tells himself there's no harm in it. That little thought becomes his reward. He'll never admit it, but being wanted, even quietly, still gives him life.

In other words:
- He doesn't go out looking for women, but he still likes to feel wanted. That small sense of power feeds his ego even when he doesn't act on it.

- His woman believes he's settled down because he's mature, but really, he's just tired of drama and effort.
- The calm she feels in him isn't always peace; it's often boredom. He's stopped chasing women, but he hasn't started chasing growth.

When he's stressed, bored, or disconnected at home, he sometimes wanders, not to other women, but to his phone. Late at night, he scrolls, he looks, he remembers. He watches pornography more now than ever, convincing himself it's harmless. It's his way of touching sin without touching anyone.

He calls it control. He says, *"At least I'm not out there anymore."* But every time he gives in privately, he reinforces the same weakness quietly. He's not chasing women, but he's still chasing the same feeling.

Spiritually, he's not tempted by chaos anymore; he's tempted by comfort. His prayers are few. He thanks God for keeping him stable but never asks to be transformed. His peace is passive, not earned.

He's not proud of who he was, but he's not fully healed either. He lives somewhere between repentance and relapse, faithful enough to seem changed but not surrendered enough to be free.

In other words:
- He's traded his cheating for new habits that feel safer but are just as empty. He's still feeding the same urges, only in quieter ways.
- Spiritually, he's coasting. He avoids chaos but also avoids conviction.
- He's not fighting temptation. He's just comfortable without it. And comfort has never healed anyone.

The Settler is what happens when a man stops running but never learns to stand firm. He believes he's finally found balance, but what he's really found is pause. He's a man at *rest*, not *restoration*.

He doesn't want to cheat. He doesn't plan to cheat. But if temptation ever appears at the right time, in the right place, when his guard is down, his weakness might wake up again.

For now, he looks faithful, and he is, in a limited way. But true faithfulness isn't built on exhaustion; it's built on surrender. He's not chasing women anymore. He's not chasing peace either. He's simply waiting.

And that waiting ends when a man finally decides to stop living in between sin and silence. That's when he becomes *The Monk*.

THE MONK

The Monk is the man who has finally stopped cheating, not because he ran out of options but because he ran out of desire. The thrill that once drove him doesn't pull him anymore. The same opportunities that once tempted him now feel pointless.

He isn't pretending to be strong; he's learned strength through repetition. He's said no to enough moments that used to own him. Every rejection built a muscle. Every time he turned away from temptation, he took back control.

This man doesn't just wake up one day disciplined. It started with small things, his morning routines, his workouts, his diet, his prayer time, his focus. He learned that if he could stay loyal to his schedule, he could stay loyal to his woman. His discipline didn't come from guilt. It came from order.

He's not moved by lust anymore. His energy has shifted. Years of saying no and choosing restraint have changed his chemistry. His libido isn't gone, but it's calmer. His testosterone isn't wild like it used to be. He's more in control of himself physically, mentally, and spiritually.

Typically, these men are older or more mature in years. But it's not exclusive to men of great age. Time slowed them down, but wisdom refined them. When you've chased enough women, you realize every "new" body starts to feel the same. As rapper, Drake once said, *"Once you slept with one dime man, you slept with them all"*

In other words:

- He's not fighting desire every day; he's changed his appetite. What once excited him now exhausts him.
- His peace didn't come overnight; it came from years of consistent habits and saying no.
- He's learned that discipline is the real proof of manhood, not how many women he can attract, but how many he can ignore.

The Monk is still a man. He sees beauty, he notices temptation, but he doesn't move on it. He recognizes it for what it is: a test.

When a woman flirts with him at work, he doesn't flirt back. He smiles, says something polite, and walks away. When a woman messages him online, he doesn't open it twice. When he's out with friends and someone tries to get close, he makes it clear with his tone and his body language that he's not available. He doesn't toy with temptation just to prove he can say no; he avoids it altogether.

At home, his woman feels that difference. There's no sneaky behavior, no weird gaps in attention, no phone guarding. He doesn't need to hide anything because there's nothing to hide. That's a different peace.

But his woman might notice something else too, he's calmer, sometimes too calm. He doesn't always crave her physically like before. His libido has slowed, and while he still loves her deeply, his drive isn't fueled by lust anymore. He'll hug her before he grabs her. He'll hold her hand instead of her waist. In few cases, he has to learn true intimacy again after years of running on pure lust.

In other words:
- This man doesn't prove faithfulness through silence; he proves it through habits that leave no room for secrets.
- His woman may mistake peace for boredom, not realizing his calm is his control.
- His love isn't cold; it's matured. It's not fueled by lust anymore; it's grounded in intimacy.
-

There are two kinds of Monks. One finds his discipline through faith; the other through structure.

The first one is spiritual. His transformation started with faith. He remembers the guilt, the shame, the emptiness that came after cheating. When he surrendered to God, he found peace that women could never give him. Every day, he renews that choice, not because he's scared of sin but because he finally respects himself.

You'll find him in church, Bible in hand, head bowed. When he speaks about love, he doesn't just talk about romance; he talks about grace, mercy, and restoration. He knows that cheating isn't just a betrayal of his woman; it's a betrayal of the God who saved him.

The second Monk doesn't quote scripture, but he lives by a code. He built his own religion; discipline. His structure is sacred. He eats clean, wakes early, trains hard, plans everything. He replaced temptation with repetition.

He's the man who started with small wins, staying consistent in the gym, cutting off bad habits, cleaning up his finances. The more he learned to control the

little things, the easier it became to control the big
ones.

In other words:

- One Monk stays faithful to God. The other
  stays faithful to his system.
- Both found power in structure, one through
  prayer, the other through purpose.
- For both, faithfulness isn't about denying
  women; it's about denying weakness.

These men still feel temptation sometimes, but they
process it differently. When they notice another
woman, they don't fantasize. They remind themselves
of what's at stake. When their old urges rise, they
redirect them, into work, exercise, prayer, or presence.

He knows that giving in even once would undo years
of work. And he's not willing to lose peace for
pleasure again.

At home, he's present. He spends time with his
woman. He pays attention. He listens. Their
relationship may not have wild passion every night,

but it's consistent. He's emotionally available now in ways he never was when he lived in lust.

He doesn't chase new women. He chooses the same one again and again.

But sometimes his woman wonders what happened to the spark. She misses the fire, the chase, the heat of early love. But what she doesn't always see is that this calm version of him is what it took to have a faithful one.

The wildness that used to make him exciting was the same wildness that made him unstable. The quiet man she has now is the same one who chose her over his impulses. He's not the man he used to be, and that's exactly the point.

He's loyal. He's present. He's peaceful.

He no longer needs the world's attention, only his woman's respect. He's not searching for women. He's protecting the woman he finally doesn't want to lose. He's not running from temptation. He's walking in control. He's not chasing love. He's living in it.

If you've ever loved a man who's been through the four stages before this, you'll understand that peace like his isn't weakness, it's victory. And while he may seem to have lost some edge, he hasn't lost sight of you.

CHEATING: 103

The Fruit

Now that you've seen the stages, let's talk about you. Have you been cheated on? If so, what did you do about it? What did he do about it? How did you find out? Who was it with?

Every situation is different, but one thing stays the same: cheating is a choice. Even when it's *revenge cheating,* it's still a choice. There's no excuse for it. There's always another option. But many people are slaves to their emotions. They feel hurt, so they want their partner to hurt too.

The truth is, once we learn to be *slaves* to a higher power instead of our lower emotions, we can thrive. Real growth begins when we stop being controlled by our feelings and start mastering them.

There are many reasons a man may step out, but they all begin inside him. The fight isn't between you and your man; it's within him - between his spirit and his mind. That's the quiet war you don't see.

When he says he loves you, he might genuinely feel that he does. Because for him, subconsciously, cheating has nothing to do with you. It's between him, the other woman, and his temptation - the battle he's either fighting or completely ignoring.

I tell women all the time: ask your man about the temptations he faces. Question him about the silent wars he's fighting within himself. He may actually need your help - but like many men, he doesn't know how to ask for it.

But then there are the other men - the ones too far gone. Their cheating isn't a war against temptation; it's a war alongside it. They've given up the fight. Some never fought at all.

Remember this: a cheating man is a weak man. Understand that clearly.

Being controlled by your lower self is weakness. When you hear about a man who cheats, or even a woman who cheats, you're hearing about someone who's weak - someone who lacks control.

You may have been one of those people before. I hope you've grown stronger since. Because when you're not in control of yourself, you have to ask: who is?

Cheating doesn't just hurt emotionally - it can hurt physically. Literally.

I've seen men catch diseases and suddenly pull away from their women, pretending they just *"need space."* In reality, they're waiting for the infection to fade. Imagine that. The same man who said he loved her risking both of their lives just to feel good for a few minutes.

Cheating comes in many forms and wears many faces. From the guy sitting outside his mistress's house lying to his girlfriend before he walks in. To the husband *working overtime* while he's sleeping with his coworker. To the man secretly sleeping with his girlfriend's sister. To the stepfather getting too close to his stepdaughter.

All of them have inner work to do. Until they do it, no amount of vagina, no amount of oral pleasure, no amount of love will fix the *lack* of control they have over their lower selves.

So when you've been cheated on, where does that leave you?

Every woman's situation is different. Some have financial ties. Some have children. Some can walk away without looking back. But at the end of the day, it all comes down to one question:

How much is too much?

How much pain are you willing to take before you finally walk away?

And then comes the next question: how much is he willing to change? Is he ready to take back control of his urges? Is he man enough to fight temptation instead of feeding it? Is he ready to stop letting lust control him and start controlling himself? Because when a man conquers lust, he conquers cheating.

Cheating starts long before he even met you. At the end of it all, a man doesn't stop cheating because of who he's with. He stops because of who he decides to become.

Thank You

Thank you for reading *The 4 Stages of a Cheating Man.*

This book was written to give you insight into the male mind and the journey many men go through before they finally learn discipline. My hope is that it answered a few questions, and reminded you that awareness is power.

If this book gave you clarity or simple enjoyment, share it with someone who needs it. Each conversation helps another woman see the truth for herself.

- Manuel V. Johnson

Continue the Conversation

Your story matters. If you have questions about your relationship, need understanding, or simply want to share your thoughts after reading this book, I'd love to hear from you.

Scan the QR code below with your phones camera and send your message directly:

Excerpt from *Know Thy Man*
By Manuel V. Johnson

The Greatest Trick

"In navigating relationships, men often employ a subtle tactic - what I call The Greatest Trick - especially when faced with women seeking something serious. Many times, men may not even realize they're doing it.

The trick involves making a woman feel loved while simultaneously creating uncertainty about commitment. In other words, show her you love her, but tell her you don't. It may sound counterintuitive, but it's a powerful dynamic that makes it challenging for women to break away from men who have clearly stated they're not interested in a serious relationship.

Have you ever wondered why relationships that start off great often take a downward turn over time? This can possibly be a shift from the initial Make her love me phase to the complacency of I know she loves me; I don't have to try anymore. This shift can lead women to settle for less, accepting a mindset of He doesn't want a relationship, so I'll take what I can get. Often this "what I can get" is limited to casual sex and laughter.

If you find yourself dealing with a guy who has shown disinterest in a relationship, and you're contemplating waiting for him to be ready, that's your decision. However, if you're tired of hearing excuses for his lack of commitment, consider making a change in a different direction. Treat him like a friend if he verbally claims to want friendship - no physical involvement, just conversation - or even more powerfully, reclaim control of your life and move on."

To continue reading, scan below

A Prayer for Her

Heavenly Father,
I come to You carrying what I was never meant to carry
alone. Heal the wounds I tried to hide, the nights I cried in
silence, and the questions that still live in my chest.
Remind me that betrayal did not break my worth - it
revealed my strength.

Where lies once lived, let truth take root. Where pain tried
to harden me, let grace soften me. Teach me to see love
through Your eyes, not through my wounds. Replace the
chaos in my spirit with clarity. Replace confusion with
calm. Replace fear with faith.

When I start to question my value, whisper that I am still
chosen. When I am tempted to chase what left me empty,
pull me back to purpose. Guard my heart from men who
speak to my loneliness but not to my soul. Let
discernment be my protection, wisdom my weapon, and
peace my proof of healing.

And when love finds me again, let it find me whole - not
waiting to be saved, but already standing in the strength
You restored within me.

Amen.

A Prayer for Him

Heavenly Father,
I come before You with a heart that has strayed. I have broken trust, misused love, and dishonored the gift of loyalty You placed within me. I confess that I have chased validation over virtue, and moments of pleasure over purpose.

Forgive me for every heart I have wounded and every lie I've spoken to protect my pride. Teach me to face myself without excuses. Strip me of the arrogance that hides behind charm and the weakness that disguises itself as strength.

Help me rebuild what deceit has destroyed - first within me, then with those I've hurt. Restore in me the man You designed me to be: one of honor, restraint, and integrity. Replace my hunger for attention with a hunger for truth. Replace lust with love, and impulse with intention.

When temptation calls, remind me of what's at stake. When guilt whispers, remind me that redemption is still possible. Let discipline guide my hands, let honesty guide my words, and let grace guide my steps.

I no longer want to be the man who hides. I want to be the man who heals.

Amen.

Proverbs 6:32–33 (NIV)

"But a man who commits adultery has no sense; whoever does so destroys himself. Blows and disgrace are his lot, and his shame will never be wiped away."

"A man is only as faithful as his options."

- Legendary Comedian, Chris Rock

Let's hope we change that….